NATURAL LAW

MORALITY AND OBEDIENCE

BEN WOOD JOHNSON, PH.D.

TESKO
TESKO PUBLISHING
Eduka Solutions
Middletown, Pennsylvania

Natural Law: Morality and Obedience

Ben Wood Johnson, Ph.D.

EDUKA SOLUTIONS

NATURAL LAW

Morality and Obedience

By
BEN WOOD JOHNSON, PH.D.

— Dedication —

To the "fulgurant" and the intrepid Rudy

This text is also dedicated to those who strive to a better living experience. It is dedicated to those who are incarcerated, demonized, admonished, ostracized, and vilified because of their nature.

"The law is what we make of it; we are also what the law makes of us."

BWJ/May 2017

TABLE OF CONTENTS

PREFACE

This book is part of a collection of short essays dedicated to law and nature. The present installment is about natural law. Although in theory the notion of natural law contradicts the idea known as positive law, in legal obligation (or in practice), any distinction, if it were to exist at all, would be negligible.

The book begins with an introductory segment that sets the stage for the debate. The manuscript contains four sections and nine chapters. The sections include: (1) Reason and natural law; (2) The essence of laws in society; (3) The role of "Reason" in legal obedience; and (4) The nature of obligation.

The first section includes chapters 1 and 2. They are focused on the origins of legal obedience. These chapters introduce the idea of divinity and law. The goal is to sketch the role of God in setting up a framework for law and punishment in society.

The second section includes chapters 3 and 4; they discuss the true meaning of the term "Law." They explore legal obligations. Chapter 4 elaborates on the practical implications of laws in society.

The third section includes chapters 5 and 6. They examine the role of reason, morality, and social rules in fomenting obedience in humans. The notion of obligation is debated based on the views espoused by prominent legal philosophers and political theorists.

The fourth section includes chapters 7, 8, and 9. These chapters explore the facets of the theory of obligation while elaborating on the term obedience. The chapters discuss the contradictions in the literary discourse. They examine the role of morality in obligation while summarizing the arguments echoed throughout the manuscript.

The conclusion restates the initial thesis of the text. There is an irrefutable distinction between the laws of men and the laws of nature. The theme echoed throughout the manuscript is that there is always an obligation to the law.

The book does not expand on the notion of obedience. It does not reflect the extent of citizen duties in society. Another publication is more in-depth on the subject. Refer to the text titled *"Legal Obligation"* to learn more.

NATURAL LAW

The present edition is more restrictive. It examines the degree to which natural law could explain the reason people may feel obligated to obey laws while exploring the need for legal obedience. But the book is not without limits.

Despite the insights proposed here, the text is limited in scope. It only examines the issues from a narrow perspective. Keep these parameters in mind as you navigate this volume.

June 6, 2017
Ben Wood Johnson, Ph.D.

Updated January 2023

NATURAL LAW

ACKNOWLEDGMENTS

THE AUTHOR WANTS TO THANK those who contributed to completing this work. He wishes to express his thanks to Paul Dégrange, Charlaze Moulin, and Karolin Viola Fritz-Gerald, for their valuable feedback and other comments on parts or in all facets of this compilation. Thanks to the editing team at Tesko Publishing for taking the time to revise and update the manuscript. Thanks to Wood Oliver for taking the time to polish the present edition. Thank you all.

NATURAL LAW

Keywords: law, morality, reason, natural law, positive law, and political obligation

INTRODUCTION

Life would be less complicated if humans had not complicated their living experience.

BWJ 2017

This book builds on a number publication that many thinkers in political philosophy or legal jurisprudence have authored over the years. It includes works by Lysander Spooner, Herbert Lionel Adolphus Hart (known as H. L. A. Hart), John Austin, Joseph Raz, Alexander Passerin d'Entrèves, and Hans Kelsen, just to name a few. Although the views outlined here apply to the debate about legal obligation, the text does not poise itself as the only point of reference on the subject.

The views echoed in the present context are not the result of random reflections. This is an excerpt of a larger body of work that I compiled many years ago. The book is not a way to vent personal frustrations. This work was compiled hoping to discuss drawbacks in the literature.

There is little or no correlation between the laws of nature (properly understood, natural law) and the laws of men (properly stated, positive law) with legal obligation. The book echoes a parallel worldview about prevalent opinions. It offers an alternative analysis.

This work is a critical analysis of the term "legal obligation." It does not go into the "nitty-gritty" of the issues that could arise from the practicality of the term itself. After making this observation, the text offers a succinct but thorough examination of the implications of nature, society, law, obligation, and politics. This perspective is a simplified version of the debate.

A Better Approach to Natural Law

The concept known as natural law is complex. Examining it requires a sensible approach. Sadly, this is not the reality of the present discourse. The argument is that we must do better when exploring the term natural law.

Another contention is that there is a need for a more coherent approach to the subject. There is also a need for a unique slant in the debate. The notion of legal obedience requires a thoughtful examination of the issues that make up the literature.

In this softback, the hope is to explain the intricacies of the debate. The pervading belief is that there is a plain difference between the laws of the natural and the laws made by men. However, this work offers a different approach. Although this work was not designed to argue that man-made laws are like natural laws, it refutes popular presumptions about the perceived differences that characterize the debate.

Indeed, natural laws and manufactured laws are not the same. However, an epistemological difference is worthy of note. There is little or no intellectual variance between *manmade* or *artificial* laws (properly stated, positive laws) and *natural* laws (properly stated, the laws of nature). But this is the case, as these terms are now understood. There is a need to recenter the conversation.

Most researchers do not examine the subject helpfully. Most people cannot grasp the gist of the problems. We could describe many of the views that pervade the literature as misguided (if not inaccurate). The intellectual undergarments of the term natural law are not convincing enough to gratify the inquisitive inclination of most observers, including myself, to discover the truth about the underpinnings of laws in society.

The literature is not exhaustive enough to support what we know (or what we understand now) about natural law is all there is to know. My curiosity about legal obligation led me to so many questions, many of which the literature has yet to clarify. This work fills that literary gap, an intellectual chasm that is widening further each day.

Although in theory most scholarly works project a clear delineation between natural law and positive law, this difference, if it were to exist at all, would be insignificant. Interpretations about the notion known as natural law (properly stated, the laws of nature) are often based on misinterpreted notions. Pointing out that a man's ability to reason alone does not provide enough grounds to make the case that individual's actions come from conceptions about natural laws.

Most people equate natural law with divine law. But God's law is not necessarily similar to the laws of nature. An inconsistency in the debate is worthy of further scrutiny. But this disconnect permeates the literary debate. It has been that way for many years now. This text hopes to fill the void that permeates the literature.

Not an Exhaustive Review

This edition is not an exhaustive review of the current debate. However, it is a valuable tool for examining the issues. Although I do not explore the term natural law in depth, I assess this notion in the most simplistic manner.

It is important to explore to what extent we could understand the capacity of a person to reason as a foundation of legal obedience. We could not understand the notion of reason as the chief point of natural law or any other law.

Personal insights alone could not explain the origins of the laws of nature. A person's capacity to reason does not (or could not) account for every human behavior, including impulsive actions and calculated omissions. There is a need to explore how prominent theorists have approached the issues. There is a need to point out obvious idiosyncrasies in the debate. There is also a need to assess existing lies in the literature.

The book does not stress the many argumentative, if not logical, flaws, which characterize the literature. This is not a rebuttal of major beliefs about the law. The book does not examine the weight (or the lack of it) of legal obedience in society. Despite the mention drawbacks, this work is informative.

NATURAL LAW

SECTION 1

Reason & Natural Law

1. DIVINE LAW

Before evaluating whether there is an obligation in the law or to the law, we must first cater a good grasp of the idea (that is, law) as an independent social tool. Raymond Wacks asked, "What is this thing called law?"[1] Although this may sound like a simple question, finding the correct answers could be daunting.

Coming up with sound explanations, which might make unanimity in the debate could be difficult, if not impossible. Trying to find objective answers about laws could be a futile effort. It can be easier to make inferences about the law rather than engaging in tangible actions to prove the weight of certain legal arguments.

---

[1] Raymond Wacks, *The Philosophy of Law: A Very Short Introduction* (Oxford ; New York: Oxford University Press, 2006), xii.

NATURAL LAW

Detecting answers about what is the law could be a chimerical undertaking. Such answers are not always succinct. Accepted explanations are multifaceted and, most often, inconsistent.

This effort is to echo those ordinary views about what a law is (or such a tool could be) might be erroneous. My approach is subjective, considering the lack of empirical references presented in the present context. The literature contains many works that seek to disentangle the essence of laws in society. Since similar works can be contentious, there is enough confusion in the debate about the law or its origins.

Although we often debate what makes up a law (or what a law could be) exhaustingly, there is a uniformity about certain facets of the term. There is the belief that many diverted the law to mean certain things that are not necessarily compatible with the foundation of society. Frederic Bastiat, for instance, began his book titled *"The Law,"* by exclaiming, "The law perverted!"[2]

Instead of an introduction, Bastiat argues that the law has "not only been diverted from its proper direction," but it had been taken over by "every kind of avarice."[3] Bastiat further notes that some people distorted the mission of the law to become a tool for punishment. The problem with that view is that any law demands a punishment device if their violation. Having a

---

[2] Frederic Bastiat, *The Law* (New York, N.Y.: Cosimo Classics, 2007), 1.
[3] ibid

punishment mechanism is the essence of every law. This is true regardless of whether such a law is just.

It is not clear whether Bastiat was seeking to make a sound argument in favor of a neutral law or even an independent legal tool. Every law has its own idiosyncrasies. The issue is whether such peculiarities are (or could be) in line with what a particular social group might value and might adhere to for a long time. Any concerns about the law must center on whether members of society will live by the rules of the law that they passed or agreed to be passed, even if such a law might affect them harmfully.

Carl Schmitt points to John Locke who declared, "Law gives authority," but failed to accept that the authority that the law invests in society and does not sketch who should enjoy this authority.[4] While there is no need to challenge that view, it is not clear whether every member of society could exert the same amount of influence in either the lawmaking or the law enforcement mechanism.

If the law were to be indiscriminate toward the person enforcing it and the person whom the law affects the most, then it would not be a law. I would refer to such an instrument as a *"Caprice."* A law that does not punish is simply *not a law* in the genuine sense of the term. At any rate, what would be the purpose of the law then? Why

---

[4] Carl Schmitt and Tracy B. Strong, *Political Theology: Four Chapters on the Concept of Sovereignty*, trans. George Schwab, 1 edition (Chicago: University Of Chicago Press, 2006), 32.

would we have laws in effect in a social setting if punishment were elective?

Punishment and Law

Let us get back to examining the notion of punishment. We could not speak of law unless there is a punishment mechanism, which is attached to the law and is presently in effect for any violation thereof. Law and punishment go together. But we could not control the punishment mechanism conceived and implemented by those who created and enacted the law. It may be difficult to do the same for those who must follow the law.

Unlike those who made the law, those who must answer to the law are not free to do whatever they may please with the law. Hence, these individuals are not free from the law. They answer to both the law and its enforcers. Under similar circumstances, the law becomes a punishment mechanism, which castigates anyone who challenges its legitimacy and the authority of those who enforce said legitimacy.

The fallacy is that no one is above the law. Although this is true in theory, those who make rules are the exception to the rules they created. Hence, these people are (or they feel) above (if not beyond) the law. For example, if the police were subjected to the same laws they enforced, they would have to pay a ticket every time they give one to a speeding motorist. To catch a traffic law violator, notably a speeding motorist, the police often violate the same law, which, many times, he is enforcing. To enforce to law, more often than not, the enforcer must violate the law.

Carl Schmitt's argument is intellectually insignificant, for it reveals little about the problems that are germane to law enforcement and citizen obedience. Every law must have a punishment mechanism built into its core. In the same way, someone must first violate the law before another could enforce it. Legal violation and law enforcement go together.

Every artificial law must be enforceable. If such a legal contrivance were to be unenforceable, it would not be a law. Such an instrument can be a *"Suggestion."* There are little or no viable arguments to disagree with the notion that punishment is the essence of every law.

Because of artificial laws, we could not relegate their enforcement to the entity whose conducts fall under the law. The authority of the law always lies in those who developed it and those who enforce it.

The public (as a whole) does not make a law. Instead, members of the public elect or select those who are going to make laws on their behalf. Thus, the public (as a unit) is always subject to the laws, which a small, but selected, group of individuals passed on its behalf. Since punishment is always part of every law, the public (whether as a unit or as a group of individuals) must obey the law.

We are still stuck with the original question. What is the law? I discuss this question further in the manuscript.

Stay with me as I develop my arguments throughout the document.

Let me say right off the bat that answers referring to laws (for example, what is law, who makes laws, and who is obligated to the law) are not always succinct. The current debate is moot. It lingers on an infinite loop about laws, especially artificial laws. Modern jurisprudence is characterized by dissenting views about the essence of laws and their practicality. Let us further explore jurisprudence.

Modern Jurisprudence and Law

Modern scholars in jurisprudence often explain the term law from two major perspectives: natural law and positive law.[5] While what makes up positive law could be direct, the extent or the origin of natural laws could be hard to pin down. What is now known about natural law is perverted, as Bastiat hints.

When legal scholars speak of natural law, they are mostly not talking about the laws of nature as an intrinsic system of control within the natural environment. Rather, they focus on the notion of divinity and laws. God is the first instance of law. Such laws are natural, they say. I

---

[5] John Austin and H. L. A. Hart, *The Province of Jurisprudence Determined and The Uses of the Study of Jurisprudence* (Indianapolis, IN: Hackett Publishing Company, Inc., 1998).

disagree with that understanding. Let me elaborate further.

I am not convinced that the laws of God are the same as the laws of nature (*see* Chapter 9). The common view is that natural law is inherent in the being. Each person is endowed with the capacity to distinguish certain conducts in their utility and vanity. God himself granted that inherent human feature (the so-called) into the being.

This view is a narrow understanding of how nature works. The laws of nature do not regulate human conduct. Instead, such laws limit exchanges among species; they limit relations between human beings and external entities within the wilderness itself. Natural law (as understood) does not emanate from a need for control or a want to punish those who refuse to be subjected to such controls or similar punishments.

We could understand natural law as the manner in which nature defines certain conducts and states of beingness. However, understandings about nature and the law seldom consider the ambivalence between what is natural (that is, naturality) and what is legal (that is, legality). We seldom consider the role of nature when we speak of natural law.

We often treat the natural environment as an unpleasant environment which, from our belief, is not essential for our existence. The common belief is that we must seek nature; we must nurture the natural. By this, most people believe that the natural has little or no bearing on human beingness. But this is a foolish racket.

A popular misguided view of nature hinges on the notion that killing is wrong. Yet, men kill men all the time and for a petty reason. Men even created laws that allow them to kill each other without the possibility of moral retribution. Men use the law as a foundation for all the biases that characterize being a human being in the world.

Men often use the law as a tool to take other people's lives with little or no moral drawback. From the belief of most people, so long as their actions are based on some legal doctrine, they are acceptable. Thus, such actions should be natural. But *legality* differs from *naturality*.

Naturality Versus Legality

Although we often use the term *legality* instead (or in place) of what is normal (that is, the norm), that does not make such happenings natural. We should never mistake *the natural* for behaviors or conducts that we could consider either *legal* or *normal*. What is the norm, according to the man's understanding of normality, which is not natural? Therefore, we should not use these terminologies interchangeably.

It may be normal for a man to obey the law. But is not such behavior natural in men? What is normal is not always natural? Saying otherwise is not true.

The preceding understanding of natural law (as now understood) is a condensed version of the idea that permeates the debate. At least, this is the way I understand the current conversation about what a law is, who makes it, and for what purpose. But the views I echo in the next few pages do not reflect that intellectual paradigm. I see the law, including those who create it, those who enforce it, and those who are victimized by it under different prisms.

I do not consider, at least instrumentally, natural law as the laws of nature. Making the claim that natural law is akin to the laws of God, or the law of nature is a misguided way of looking at the issues. Nature does not have laws which men could enforce.

The laws of nature (as must be understood) are not similar to the laws of God (so understood). To make the opposite claim, one would have to presume that God is beyond nature. Put differently, God and nature would have to be two unique entities that co-exist on the same plane field, or they are the same entities that interact with the world on different plane fields.

I do not dispute that there might be a relationship between nature and God (that is, if there is God). I am uncertain whether that harmony is the foundation of all laws in nature (that is, natural laws). Natural law (as now understood) is the foundation of artificial laws. Chapter 9 notes the laws of nature are not restrictive.

Obedience to the laws that create the natural environment does not emanate from the willingness of the being to be bound, from his need to obey, from his intent to abdicate, or from his willingness to comply with any laws in effect in his or her commorancy and authority. The laws of nature are intrinsic to the being.

NATURAL LAW

The law is part of the being. But there is more to this argument. The laws of men reflect the understanding that God himself plays a prominent role in shaping human behavior.

We understand that we must reprimand or condemn all conduct that does not conform to God's expectations. We are certain that we must punish those who engage in similar conduct. This is the basis of society. Social rules are based on rewards and punishments. That reality has little or nothing to do with the laws of men.

2. SUPREMAL LAW

Recently, I coined the term "*supremal* law." I did so as an expedient intellectual means to depict the essentiality of the laws of men in nature. As the name suggests, the term *"Supremal law"* typifies the notion that the law is supreme. This law is above everything else in the natural world.

The doctrinal reason for such an approach to law is based on notions that place the *lawgiver* or the *lawmaker* above the practicality of the law itself. This is the law of laws. This is the law of everything and everyone that is not the law or is associated with the law. But this is also a selective approach to lawmaking.

A Supremal law is a law that has no boundary. This law supersedes human nature in its true essence. This is an irrational law in its most livid and most tangible forms. Yet, this is the law of humanness.

Life is structured that way; at least this is how society structures the living experience for human beings these days. We have structured living arrangements in most modern societies in such a way for many centuries now. Some might even say that this approach became the model of law for thousands of years. It is not surprising that human life is a misfortune. But it is getting even worse.

Human beings are condemned to break Supremal laws. However, we designed such laws to break human beings. Human species is the only entity in danger within the natural. But how long this would be the story of the species? The answer is not clear.

This is just a chapter in the history of the species and not necessarily the story of the species itself. Time will reveal how long this would be the reality of human beings in their world. Let us explore the notion of Supremal law make sense of it all.

Natural Law Versus Supremal Law

Unlike the notion of supremal law, natural law (as should be understood) describes a law, which we could describe as neutral, immaterial, and inconsequential. By that statement, I mean that natural law carries little or no weight; at least, this is true. Nature has no particular preference. Anyone (or anything) who can survive will survive in the natural world. The problem is that the same is not true for a social environment.

The understanding here is that the laws of nature are the laws of survival. The laws of men are the laws of the highest order. We could understand these legal tools as the laws of the *Supremal*.

The notion of supremal law provides the justifications for laws, which have little or no limit in the way they control human conduct. They are the laws of sequences and consequences. Such laws create the condition for society to function in hierarchical order. Here is the problem; the laws of nature are not hierarchical. The laws of nature are linear.

Nature is not based on an idea, which we invoke to describe as either *better than* or *higher than*. There is no superlative in nature. Since natural laws (as should be understood) are linear, they overlap.

A particular limit in nature could be mitigated or compensated for by another. Another example is that my ability to be under water is based on my stamina or my physical strength to hold my breath indefinitely. Some people could stay longer under water than others can. But that state of being is only transitory.

The inherent capacity to stay under water depends on individual strength and not individual desire. Anyone could increase their capacity to stay longer under water. On that basis, natural law is not set in stone. It is not restrictive; it is not discriminatory. It is simply natural.

NATURAL LAW

The laws of nature are facilitators for human survival. The laws of men, by contrast, are burdensome; they are intrusive; they are inhibitory. Their goal is to obstruct natural human conducts. The laws of nature could not be the same as the laws of God or the laws of men. No artificial laws could come from the laws of nature (as should be understood).

The common belief is that laws control human conduct. Human beings must respond to their nature. That nature, they say, is on par with the natural reality that the person experiences. Such a view of the role that laws play in a person's life is in error.

Obeying artificial laws is not a natural reflex. There is nothing inherent in a person leaning to obey the law. Legal obedience is not intrinsic to the being. Similar viewpoints are mistaken.

The belief that God is the creator of everything, including humans, is not far-fetched. But the view that nature is only second to God is absurd. We do not know that for sure. We could not know that with certainty or beyond any doubt.

How could there be a God without nature? Where would such a God stand? How could there be a nature without a god? These are intriguing questions. But there are no definite answers. One could only guess.

If we were to agree that there is an omnipresent and omnipotent God, we must also recognize the existence of an omnipresent and omnipotent nature. Whether nature is more potent than God is a separate question, which we could discover in a unique setting. Let us be content with the notion that there would be no god without nature.

If God is the creator, then nature is the mechanism through which God's creations are possible. For that reason, nature enjoys as much power in God's creation as God himself does. It is the case that God and nature are the same, or there is no god beyond nature itself. But this is not an *agnostic* argument. Instead, this is a mere observation, which is worth pointing out in the debate.

If there is a god, there is also a nature. The problem is that the laws of nature are not the laws of God. When we speak of God's laws, it must be clear that such laws are designed and enforced by God himself. Thus, any law or any idea of that which emanated outside nature is positive.

Whether such laws are from God or from men is unimportant, for whom is obligated by them. It must be plain is that the laws of nature (or natural law, as it might be) are unenforceable. But what might explain that assertion? It is because natural law (as should be understood) is immutable, though we could violate such laws, although temporarily.

God and Law

What role does God play in creating artificial laws? One way to answer this question is that God is the foundation of all laws in society. If we were to refer to the Christian

NATURAL LAW

Bible, we might arrive at the inescapable deduction that God set the first law when he forbade Adam and Eve from eating the apple tree in the Garden of Eden.

God also laid out the scheme for artificial laws when he punished the pair for their sin. We could trace the origin of positive laws to God himself. Hence, God and artificial laws are the same. We could not have one entity without the other.

The question worth asking here is why humanity followed this orthogonal path, even though many thinkers have sought to separate legality from divinity. Why do people agree to live under restricted conditions, such as in a social setting? Although the answers are not clear, various explanations are worthy of note.

One of such theorems is a person's capacity to distinguish right from wrong. That consideration could also be described as the notion of morality. The view is that human beings can distinguish between right and wrong. Hence, human beings understand the need to obey the law.

The common view is that the capacity of every human to reason binds the person in the social milieu. Whether you call this engagement a contract (that is, a social contract) or a commitment, it is immaterial. Still, the presupposition is that we agree, at least in our life, to be governed by the laws of others. This view is absurd.

I, for one, never agreed to become a member of society. Not that I refute the privileges and the limits that my presence in that milieu entails. In society, we have fewer means or options to be in that setting. Whether we like the milieu itself is irrelevant.

Once we are in a social setting, it is no longer up to us whether we remain in it or whether we go elsewhere. Every facet of our lives is governed by the makers of the social milieu or by the rulers of the space. Hence, we have no effective means of dissociating ourselves from the place, which we were told came about because of our consent, a consent can neither be relinquished nor controlled.

We have no actual powers over the social milieu other than the ones created by our illusions. These perceived powers are inconsequential; they are intangible; they are useless.

We have no means of escaping a social setting. We could not dissociate ourselves from that environmental reality, at least not tangibly. We are stuck there. Our actions or omissions are incumbent up the rules set forth by those who control the milieu; it is not because of our desire to be a certain way.

We are the slaves of the social space. Our nature is inconsequential in that place. We are irrelevant in that space. Our nature is meaningless. Suggesting otherwise is gullible, shortsighted, or even intellectually dishonest.

We are condemned to obey the laws and rules of the social setting in which we live. Not obeying such laws would be like committing suicide. We could describe such a premature death as committing social suicide. For these reasons, the notion of "free will" is a naïve way of looking at the world.

Being in society contradicts any notion of freedom in men. These two ideas do not coincide. Any argument to the contrary would be illogical. But this debate is for another place.

It may not be necessary to debate the role of God in artificial laws in the present text. Please see the text titled *"Crime and Nature"* to learn more about the subject. There, we elaborate further on the *"reason"* argument. But I might be inclined to do so under a subjective lens.

The Crowning Truth

A popular assumption is that there is a supreme truth in the world. That truth, many are convinced, is the divine truth. Many believe that God is the source of anything good or any state of virtue in the world. All laws must be good and just. I challenge that supposition.

Although this intellectual convention is idealistic, it is not true. God could not make *just* laws, which impute punishments for those who refuse to obey them. As the creator of all beings on earth, God should know that each being is *unique* in his own way. Imposing laws on the being which are not sentient to the being would be an *unjust* burden. God would be expected to be perfect, while he (himself) might not be.

The laws of nature (so understood and so practiced) are not the laws of God. Nature does not have laws that men could mimic or enforce. The laws of nature are not enforceable, though they are not suggestive. They are inalienable; they are sacred. Let us further assess approaches to nature and personal obligation.

Let me offer a word of caution as we continue in the debate. This book is not an atheist manifesto. It is not a denial of God (if God there is in the world of men). But to clarify the basis of artificial laws, we have to encapsulate the nature of these laws. This is also not a *Nihilist* argument. Granted, it might be difficult (if not impossible) to grasp the essence of life outside nature.

The gist of my argument here is that artificial laws, whether their names stemmed from natural law doctrines [6] or positive laws, emanate from religious beliefs. It is necessary to underline that a point of departure of all artificial laws is God himself. Even though legal positivists might argue to the contrary, every law (so long as it is not natural within the essence of the term *nature*) it is positive.

Every unnatural law is based on God's prospects. Else, such laws must reflect a man's interpretation of what God's expectations are or what they might be. Such laws must almost result from the search for righteous men. Thus, artificial laws are purposeful at their core. They are (or they must be) the laws of good versus evil.

Nature knows neither good nor bad; nature knows neither good nor evil; nature knows neither right nor

---

[6] This argument is based primarily on the present literary discourse.

wrong. If it is possible, then it is natural. If it is natural, then it is unenforceable. If it is unenforceable, then it is inherent; it is intrinsic; it is innate in the being. By it, it is not up to the being to abdicate to his or its nature to comply with a law or a natural rule.

We could not sing a similar tune to the laws of men. This is also true for the laws of God. Every unnatural law is also positive.

We should not relegate natural law, as now understood, to laws which stemmed from God himself or any idea of a religious patron of some sort, which we rise to a God-like status or a divine essence. The positive law is also a natural law, at least based on the way the current model describes this idea. In these terms, we could not exclude God or any notion of divinity from our analysis.

Understanding the Law

Certain legal ideas are complex to the untrained observer. The law in practice and the law in theory are intrinsically different. Nevertheless, a broad knowledge of legal theory or political philosophy is not a precondition to practicing the law effectively.

Legal scholars are not necessarily law practitioners. However, law practitioners do not always grasp the foundation of the legal profession and the effects of making or enforcing laws. There is a fine line that interlaces who makes laws, who enforces laws, and who are subjected to those laws. There is a fine line between the purpose of the law and the effects of the law. We also note that these realities seldom jibe with one another. Laws are not structured to benefit the public without being damaged by the public at the same time.

Applying or enforcing the law often falls within the discretion of law enforcers (that is, the police, prosecutors, and other law enforcement entities or mechanisms). Applying the law often comes from the subjective interpretation of one man (that is, a judge) or a group of men (for example, several judges or a jury).

The multifaceted nature of the term law (or legal theory) makes it impulsive to study. Therefore, we could argue that the epistemological foundations of various legal ideas result from speculations. No one knows what law is and how it came about. Within the last few centuries, a few philosophers laid out, what Leslie Green refers to as, a "blueprint" for understanding law.[7]

Scholars like H. L. A. Hart, Ronald Dworkin, John Austin, Joseph Raz, John Finnis, Heinrich Rommen, J. Budziszewski, Hegel, Leo Strauss, Yves Simon, Jacques Maritain, John Simmons, Allan Hutchinson, and Hans Kelsen—this is just to name a few—rose to prominence in the field of legal theory. We could consider their rise to stardom because of their work on law.

---

[7] Leslie Green, "Legal Obligation and Authority," in *The Stanford Encyclopedia of Philosophy*, ed. Edward N. Zalta, Winter 2012 (Metaphysics Research Lab, Stanford University, 2012), https://plato.stanford.edu/archives/win2012/entries/legal-obligation/.

NATURAL LAW

Many of these thinkers are considered the intellectual backbone of modern jurisprudence. But their views, however incomplete, inaccurate, or misguided they might be, are often embraced as the supreme authority in political philosophy or modern jurisprudence. Most modern observers do not subscribe to existing approaches to various legal ideas, including authority and obligation. The views outlined in the present context mirror facets of the claims that are often echoed by most of the mentioned thinkers.

SECTION 2

The Essence of Laws in Society

3. RECYCLED IDEAS

Despite the bewilderment that pervades the idea of obligation, there are fewer novel arguments offered by most scholars, which could explain the intellectual foundation of the idea itself. Moralists or philosophers struggled with the idea of obedience to the law. But philosophers like Socrates advanced interesting arguments in many of their works about the notion of obligation, mostly in political obligation.[8] The most prominent thinker that comes to mind here is Plato.

---

[8] In Trial and Death, Plato lays the foundation for understanding obedience, political obedience. Plato notes that his residence in Athens binds him into an agreement with the laws in effect. Because he resides there, he is committed to obey those laws. He also attributes all his possession, both intellectual and material, to the laws of Athens. He is obligated to obey them.

NATURAL LAW

In Socrates (Trial and Death), for instance, Plato laid out the foundation for understanding political obligation.[9] But this is where legal theory took the wrong turn. Plato's works are considered the intellectual basis of political philosophy or legal theory. John Finnis made the case that Plato rescued natural law from nihilist ideals.[10]

Finnis further recognizes that the term natural law does not mean what it could mean or what it should mean.[11] Plato came up with a version of the term natural law. But Plato's take is incompatible with what could be considered the laws of the natural. This inconsistency is the essence in the views that pervade the literature.

This is not to deny the role of Plato in laying down the limits of law or in setting up modern jurisprudence. This prominent thinker did not reveal everything that needed to be known about political obligation in laying down his take on natural law principles. In determining the crux of natural law ideals, the proper point of analysis should not have begun in the *Trial and Death*, as Plato explained. Rather, the actual point of analysis should center on the traits of nature. It should reflect the features of natural law, which can be unequivocal.

There is no need to address natural law passionately in this context. The idea of natural law (or the laws of

---

[9] Green, "Legal Obligation and Authority."

[10] Oxford Conversations, *What Is New Classical Natural Law Theory?*, John Finnis: Life of Faith, 2016, https://www.youtube.com/watch?v=0N5ffOMBOZc.

[11] Ibid.

nature) is complex. It is important to elaborate on the current social, political, and legal understandings of what law is or what it should be.

Current approaches to obedience might make little or no sense to anyone who wants to understand what makes up a legal obligation in society. It is unlikely that there is an enormous difference between natural law (as now understood) and positive law (as currently defined). The present debate on this issue is perverted.

The difference that many scholars often seek to set up between the two notions is intellectually inconsequential. So long as that distinction is based on the laws of men and the laws of God, it would be analytically unimportant. God is the product of a man's thirst for confirmation in the wilderness or in nature.

The natural law, in its true essence and as men understand it, is not the law of God, at least if God is an independent entity. The natural law entails the laws of nature. God's law, at least in the way men understand it, is a positive law. There is no tangible way to quantify (or even qualify) God's law. Assuming that there is a god, his law (or supposing that) must result from a subjective interpretation of his intents. God's law is also men's law, for men are the sole carriers of God's law.

The literature about natural law is complex. It is also filled with ideas that are contradictory. Many of the views that pervade the debate are redundant. This makes the conversation about natural law ambiguous. It is not surprising that views about "what is law" or what law can be may also be reflected by intense debates.

Defining the Term "Law"

The definitions of the term "law" in its most simplistic sense vary in both substance and content. Many schools of thought claim to define the law by how it is practiced, who makes it, how it is applied (or enforced), and who must obey laws. However, what is understood about the characteristics of law could easily become inaccurate as time elapses.

Contentions about certain legal approaches are constantly under scrutiny; legal definitions are often changed or challenged by new definitions. With leading theories on legal ideas, namely *"man-made"* laws, explanations usually depend on short-lived assessments or even speculations. This is to echo the idea that definitions of what makes up the law often reveal argumentative discrepancies in the debate.

What do we know about the law often change depending on the social context in which a particular law is being assessed or defined? Viewpoints about the notion of law are ephemeral. Legal doctrines do not always survive the test of time.

Lord Denning notes that principles of law that suited to the social conditions of a particular time may not meet the social needs and the social opinion of a different time.[12] Principles of law must be molded and shaped to meet the needs and the opinions of contemporaneous times.[13] Thus, we could examine the law from various angles.

The Different Angles of Laws

We could understand the law from various models. We could view the law as a structure; we could view it as a mechanism; we could view it as a tool.

As a structure, the law could become the pillars of the social institutions they created to solidify. As a mechanism, the law could become the framework that tells, shapes, and guides social practices. The law could become a reference point for moral notions that regulate social practices.

The law could become an integral part of society. As a tool, the law could become a device that helps in performing various social tasks. One of the fundamental features of the law, regardless of time or location, is that all laws create consequences for actions or inaction.

John Austin argues that laws are defined, understood, and practiced as commands.[14] In the book titled "*The Province of Jurisprudence Determined and The Uses of the Study of*

---

[12] Alfred Denning, *The Discipline of Law*, 1 edition (London: Oxford University Press, 2005).

[13] Ibid.

[14] Austin and Hart, *The Province of Jurisprudence Determined and The Uses of the Study of Jurisprudence.*

Jurisprudence," Hart points out that we could understand the Austin doctrine in the following manner.

> "Laws properly so called are defined as commands which oblige a person or persons to a course of conduct and the 'essential difference' of positive law is found to be that it is set by a sovereign to the members of an independent political society."[15]

The previous statement suggests that the mere presence of laws or the mere existence of the law creates duties. Such duties are always binding; thus, they are non-optional. The law is a forerunner to obligation, and not the other way around.

Law as a Requirement

A law, by its most formal characterization, is a requirement. It could be a non-optional social requirement. No one is supposed to be above the law. Under the notion of equality, every member of society must obey all the laws and all the rules in effect. Such laws or similar rules must apply evenly across the board.[16]

Here is the sad truth; most laws do not always apply evenly. Not every member of society sees the law through the same lens. Those who enforce the law seldom do so

---

15 Ibid., 10.

16 Green, "Legal Obligation and Authority."

from a neutral lens. Some people are above the law, although few would admit that reality openly.

Let us say that some groups could be free from certain laws. Under the doctrines known as "sovereign, absolute, qualified immunity, and entities," [17] certain groups, entities, or person (or anyone)—acting within their duty—often enjoy immunity from certain laws.[18] The law does not apply to them. Otherwise, they are above the law.

To solidify a succinct definition of law, Alexander Passerin d'Entrèves further notes:

> "Law—*Ius*—is an art and a science all in one. As a science, it is knowledge of human and divine things (*divinarum atque humanarum rerum notitia*), a theory of right and wrong (*iusti atque iniusti scientia*). As an art, it is the furtherance of what is good and equitable (*ars boni et aequi*)."[19]

By inference, a law is both a tool and an instrument. As an instrument, we could use a law as means or an agency to achieve a required effect. We could consider the effect as obedience. The law could also induce other effects, namely virtue in men.

---

[17] The immunity doctrines apply to tort laws or cases involving tort liability issues.

[18] Philip Chase Tobin, *25 Doctrines of Law You Should Know* (New York: Algora Publishing, 2007).

[19] Alexander Passerin D'Entrèves and Cary J. Nederman, *Natural Law: An Introduction to Legal Philosophy* (New Brunswick, N.J: Routledge, 1994), 24.

NATURAL LAW

Cary Nederman points out that we could understand the d'Entrèvesian approach to law as a search for "moral rectitude." [20] Other observers also believe that the purpose of law "is not only to make men obedient, but to help them be virtuous. [21] That brings us to an interesting question. What is the essence of laws in society? Are there laws to improve men or society?

The Purpose of Laws

Leslie Green argues, "Laws and legal systems are not a matter of nature but artifice."[22] Laws are outside nature itself. Green further notes that laws are "social constructions."[23] To put this understanding in a broader context, let us say that laws are artificial devices, which we (humans) tailored to advance a particular agenda. That agenda is obedience. The laws of men are always purposeful (*see* Chapter 2).

It is unlikely that compulsion is not an intrinsic facet of the law. Leslie Green notes, "The idea that law is essentially a coercive apparatus resonates with the layperson's view and has been popular in

---

[20] Ibid., xix.
[21] Alessandro Passerin d'Entrèves, *Natural Law: An Introduction to Legal Philosophy*, 2nd ed. (London: Hutchinson University Library, 1970), 82., as cited in D'Entrèves and Nederman, *Natural Law*, xix.
[22] H. L. A. Hart et al., *The Concept of Law*, 3 edition (Oxford, United Kingdom: Oxford University Press, 2012), xvii.
[23] Ibid.

jurisprudence."[24] It is not clear what idea Green meant to convey here.

There is no need to dispute the view that a legal duty is only a final mechanism, which is built into the law itself. But a few observers believe that sanctions are not the primary purpose of the law. Rather, they are "the law's Plan B."[25] They only apply if the subjects of the law do not "conform to the law without further supervision."[26] This view makes no sense at all. Later in the text, I explain why.

The law is a tool. We could use it as a device, so crafted to perform a task, so made up to allow the individual to perform an operation; it is also there to make it possible to conduct a goal. We could use the law to induce the obedience of citizens. A sense of virtue is necessary to behave in such a manner. By relying on the d'Entrèvesian approach to law, the view is that the law "is inescapably embedded in the realm of moral values."[27]

Gerald and Kathleen Hill define law as "Any system of regulation to govern the conduct of the people of an organization, community, society, or nation."[28] By that logic, a law could be "A statute, ordinance, or regulation enacted by the legislative branch of government."[29]This

---

[24] Ibid., xxx.

[25] Ibid.

[26] Ibid.

[27] D'Entrèves and Nederman, *Natural Law*, xix.

[28] Gerald Hill, Kathleen Hill, and Nolo Editors, *Nolo's Plain-English Law Dictionary*, 1 edition (Berkeley, CA: NOLO, 2009), 244.

[29] Ibid.

definition implies that anyone who lives within a group or the people who engage in activities in an organization, a society, a community, or a nation must obey the law.

The laws are for a particular purpose. This is the purpose of control. Laws always create duties. To that effect, people are expected to obey the law. We could explain this understanding by evoking the term, "No one is above the law." But obedience to the law is not automatic.

A legal obligation must be imposed; it must be enforced. The notion that people should conform to the law "without further supervision" is inaccurate; at least, this is not the case.

Other accounts about laws suggest that we could use laws as tools to create documents.[30] We could use those documents, as guidance for sanctions and schemes for social structures. The intrinsic value of any law (or the irrefutable function of any law) is the inducement of obedience.

To achieve this, every law has a sanction. Hans Kelsen notes that a law's primary function is to create sanction.[31] A law that creates sanctions is also a law that enforces duties.

If duties demand enforcement, then they are not necessarily inherent features of society; they are not inherent in men. The need for sanctions undermines the

---

[30] Denning, *The Discipline of Law.*

[31] Hans Kelsen, *General Theory of Law And State*, 1 edition (Clark, N.J: The Lawbook Exchange, Ltd., 2007), 69.

notion of consent. Duties are neither dependent on the want of the individual nor on the results of an inherent characteristic in human beings to comply with laws. The logical conclusion is that laws are intrinsically coercive.

How could we examine the coercive nature of laws and their enforcement? We could look at the symbols of the law. The police, for example, represent the law. We could view their presence in a community as a source of obedience and compulsion. Let us explore the practical implications of laws in society from a law enforcement angle.

NATURAL LAW

4. THE PRACTICAL POWER
OF LAWS

Most police officers carry a badge, which reinforces their legitimacy and their authority to enforce the law. Unless the officer is dressed in plain clothing, his presence in the community is always distinct. For example, patrol officers carry guns; they carry tasers; they carry batons; they have radio or other forms of communication, which are inherent to their functions and their tasks.

The people are always recognizable. Police officers are always dressed in uniforms. The police travel in marked vehicles or squad cars, which feature the color and the name of the city or town they represent.

The police logo is one of the most recognizable signs in the world. The commonly known title *"The Police"* is recognizable, even when written or pronounced in a foreign language. The title *"Police"* is commonly used by law enforcement agencies around the world.

There are ninety popular languages in the world.[32] Where these languages are spoken, the police are known under similar titles. No matter where you go, identifying a police officer is not that difficult. You may spot a police officer within minutes, chiefly if the individual were to be on duty and had been dressed properly (that is, in uniform).

The presence of a police officer in uniform is not the subject of our discussions. But we could say that a police presence alone symbolizes the law. It is a reminder to citizens that the law imposes restrictions or certain limits in their conduct.

Many law enforcers believe that the mere fact that they represent the law means that the citizenry has no immediate power over their authority. However, most officers often feel the need to reiterate their authority in the way they communicate with the citizenry. Some officers often feel the need to remind the citizenry that they (that is, the police) are in charge. Under a similar

---

[32] These languages do not include dialects and other idioms. There are many more spoken languages in the world today. Stephen Anderson, for instance, has identified at least 6,909 distinct languages. See *"How many languages are there in the world?"* to learn more. Stephen R. Anderson, "How Many Languages Are There in the World?," 2010, https://www.linguisticsociety.org/content/how-many-languages-are-there-world.

regime, obedience is always expected. The citizen must obey the police authority.

Problems often arise when police officers face individuals who have no respect for the law and no respect for law enforcers. We say that these individuals often have no considerations for the well-being of the community. Confrontations between the police and the citizenry can be unavoidable. But insensitive police officers often play a role in annoying the citizen.

Power of Laws

Suppose that a citizen is stopped (or pulled over) by the police for a traffic violation. If the police officer approached the situation with a power-of-law mindset and if the citizen rebuked the officer's assertive authority, the outcome of that battle could be unpredictable. The officer would always have an edge.

Police officers are always prepared to confront uncooperative citizens. Sometimes, they do so anyway they can. As a police cadet, I remember being told by several police instructors that, an exemplary officer must live by two sets of laws: the laws on the books and the laws on the streets.[33]

The inference here is that there are situations where only the officer has the discretion to discover the best

---

[33] For a good portion of my youth, I was a patrol officer. Part of my police training took place in Fort Leonard Wood, Missouri (1995).

course of action. In such situations, the police officer becomes *"The Law"* or he acts. Sometimes, a police officer may require the citizen to obey both the law and the authority that the law awards to the officer himself.

Police have some discretion on how to enforce the law. Law enforcers, such as the police, often have some wiggle room or some latitude about how the law applies, where it applies, to whom it applies, and under which circumstance the law applies.

The culture that pervades many law enforcement organizations or entities is that a police officer must be prepared to deal with any situation and in any social setting. A weak police officer is someone who loses control of the situation. A police officer cannot afford to be made out as weak, not when the backup is a radio transmission away or a phone call away.

There is an "us versus them" mindset in various police entities. The police, as an institution or as an organization, often see its members as individuals whose rights must be protected at all costs, even if it means that someone else's rights could be undermined in the same context. From the perspective of most law enforcers, an obligation to obey is always expected from the citizenry. Therefore, the police have little or no patience for unruly citizens. If that *de facto* reality does not induce an obligation, I do not know what else will.

Extent of Obligation

An obligation is always a "binding commitment."[34] But any binding commitment would also require consent from all the parties involved. Merriam-Webster's Collegiate Dictionary, for example, notes that any obligation or compulsory activity is binding with the law or conscious.[35]

The problem here is that an obligation to the law may quash any sense of consent or individual will. Hart writes, "The most prominent general feature of law at all times, and places are that its existence means that certain kinds of human conduct are no longer optional, but in some sense obligatory."[36]

Conforming to legal duties is not necessarily the result of citizen consent to obey every law whenever confronted by the law. Rather, the citizen is always expected to comply with the law. Failing to do so could have many results for the citizen or for the individuals associated with that person.

Hart suggests that, always and in all places, laws outweigh any other considerations, including the capacity

---

[34] John Finnis, *Natural Law and Natural Rights*, 2 edition (Oxford ; New York: Oxford University Press, 2011), 297.

[35] Merriam-Webster's Collegiate Dictionary (11th Ed.) defines obligation actions that obligates oneself to a course of action (as by a promise or vow). Obligation is something one is bound to do. It could be a duty or a responsibility. Merriam-Webster, *Merriam-Webster's Collegiate Dictionary, 11th Edition*, 11th edition (Springfield: Merriam-Webster, Inc., 2003).

[36] Hart et al., *The Concept of Law*, 6.

NATURAL LAW

or the willingness of the individual to decide what, when, to whom, how, or why he or she must perform or omitted to perform a particular act or to engage in a behavior or to omit a certain conduct. Hart's take on what sets up law notes the contradiction that permeates legal theory.

One could not speak of an obligation within the same context as the notion of consent. Obligation contradicts consent. That way, consent nullifies any presumption that an obligation is optional. There could be no obligation in the presence of consent.

Consent requires a will. However, an obligation is independent of a will. Thus, an obligation could be irrevocable. Consent, nonetheless, always (and in all places) is revocable. Thus, the notion of a legal obligation puts side by side the most essential element of consent. Here, it is a "will."

The assumption is that individuals are predisposed, because of their ability to "reason," to obey just laws. This tendency creates an inherent need to do the *"right thing."* Since most laws are passed under the penumbra of justice, an unconditional obedience to said laws would *"always"* be the right thing to do.

The previous understanding undercuts the notion of consent or will. Spooner notes, "Each man shall abstain from doing, to another, anything which justice forbids him to do, as, that he shall abstain from committing theft, robbery, arson, murder, or any other crime against the person or property of another."[37] The presumption is that it is up to the individual to limit the self from engaging in bad conducts. This argument also put into question the notion that the individual enjoys the decision to do or to omit from doing.

Spooner's approach to obligation suggests that, under justice or under the moral framework, what is just for one person is also just for all people. By relying on that viewpoint, the obligation is never with expressed consent. Rather, consent is always assumed. Similarly, a person is always obliged to obey. Every human being has an irrevocable obligation to uphold all laws, whether such laws are just.

Imposing Duties

If the law imposes duties anywhere and anytime, then a person is always obligated to obey the law; this is true regardless of that person's want or wish to do otherwise. It is not always clear whether that obligation depends on the existence of the law or whether there is an inherent obligation, which calls for the existence of a law. It is not always clear whether duties create laws or whether laws create duties.

---

[37] Lysander Spooner, *Natural Law, Or, The Science of Justice: A Treatise on Natural Law, Natural Justice, Natural Rights, Natural Liberty, and Natural Society: Showing ... Is an Absurdity, a Usurpation, and a Crime.* (Place of publication not identified: Gale, Making of Modern Law, 2010), 5–6.

NATURAL LAW

With legal obligation, the views have diverged. For some observers, there is always a duty to obey the law; but for others, such a duty is ambiguous.[38] Raymond Wacks, for instance, notes, "It is rare to find supporters of the view that the duty to obey is absolute."[39] Still, whether implicitly or directly, the presumption is that there is always an obligation to obey the law. The law always brings about obligation and, in all places (*see* Chapter 3).

This is not to belabor the point. The fundamental question one must pose here is whether any law specifically creates an obligation to obey or whether there is an inherent obligation to comply with the formulae of the law. We could approach this question from two angles.

If we were to approach the concept from a natural law paradigm, the answer would stem from the instance or the entity that the law seeks to govern. Nature does not obligate anyone or anything outside the purview of the natural environment. Anything that is natural must also be unenforceable within the natural milieu itself.

Contrastingly, if we were to approach the previous question by relying on the laws of men, the answer could be more complex. This reality would lead to a "*chicken and egg dilemma.*" We would have to ask which comes first:

---

[38] Green, "Legal Obligation and Authority."

[39] Raymond Wacks, *Understanding Jurisprudence: An Introduction to Legal Theory*, 2nd edition (Oxford ; New York: Oxford University Press, 2009), 318.

the law or the obligation to obey the law? The answer might be difficult to find out.

Neither the concept of natural law nor the idea known as positive law offers enough epistemological grounds to answer the earlier question. Natural law theorists might argue that the obligation to obey the law lies in the fixed norms and values, which are guided by reason or morality. The problem is that the meaning of the term "reason" is often lost in semantics. Let us examine this idea further.

NATURAL LAW

SECTION 3

The Role of Reason in Legal Obedience

5. REASON AS SELF-CONSCIOUS ACTS

The term reason is complex. We could understand it as a reason for a person to impute his or her actions or conducts. Joseph Raz speaks of the term reason as self-conscious acts. Raz describes *"reason"* people recognize the authority of those they must obey.[40] He claims that a person uses reason as a mechanism to appraise social roles.

Raz's approach suggests that a person's view on authority results from the meanings he or she attached to such authority.[41] Because of reason, assumedly, a person may be inclined to forego his or her private judgment in

---

[40] Joseph Raz, ed., *Authority* (New York: NYU Press, 1990).
[41] Ibid.

favor of an authority's discretion.[42] The idea of "individual will" play an important role in the way authority is made out. The obligation is guided by individual opinions, Raz suggests.

Raz pitifully tried to prove a clear divide between moral reasoning and morality.[43] This prominent legal theorist suggests that the two ideas are distinct. However, Raz provided little evidence to support this argument. His belief centers on the notion that *moral reasoning* is part of *morality*. Thus, it is not morality. The inference from that understanding is that moral reasoning is not necessarily the result of morality.

In the book titled *"Authority,"* Raz writes:

"On the view I would defend, there is the highest-order framework of moral reasoning (not the whole of morality) which takes us outside ourselves to a standpoint that is independent of which we are. It cannot derive its basic premises from facets of our particular and contingent starting points within the world, though it may authorize reliance on such specialized points of view if this is justified from a more universal perspective. Since individuals are very different from one another and must lead complex individual lives, the universal standpoint cannot reasonably withhold this authorization lightly."[44]

---

[42] Ibid.

[43] Ibid.

[44] Ibid., 313.

Raz's argument seems contradictory to the theory he claims to defend. It is also worthy of note that Raz does not believe that morals play a role in law. As in Raz's own assessment of positive law, one may say that the obligation does not stem from the idea of morality.

In an excerpt from his famous book, the title *Authority*, Raz indulges in the notion that individuals enjoy a certain moral discretion in recognizing authority. This account of authority and obligation also suggests that, at some point, an individual's capacity to set up or obey law is guided by an outside mechanism, which could only be morality through reason.

Raz seems reluctant to admit that his approach to legal obligation is weak or almost futile without considering the role of morality in the individual assessment of authority. Claiming that moral reasoning plays a vital role in the life of an individual, as opposed to ideals of morality, is illogical. Raz's approach does not clarify the debate.

This approach to obligation begs the following question: Could there be moral reasoning without an overarching encroachment by morality? While the answer may not be obvious, it would not be wise to hold a firm stance on this issue.

What informs moral reasoning is not clear in Raz's argument. Morality guides moral reasoning always and in all places. Natural law has a more significant imprint on Raz's legal theory than he would admit. Morality is always present in the way people assess their behavior in society.

NATURAL LAW

Morality and Objectivity

H. L. A. Hart questioned the weight of morality with objectivity. This approach to morality is inconsistent. There is no objective morality. If the idea of morality is to be understood properly, it must be clear that *objectivity* cannot be a criterion for its assessment.

Hart recognizes that morality plays a role in obligation. However, he constantly undermines his own argument. Hart constantly ponders about the role of law in society. He often asks what such a role is or what it should be (or could be). Hart argues, "Moral rules impose obligation and withdraw certain areas of conduct from the free option of the individual to do as he likes."[45]

Hart further proposes the notion that, "Not only do law and morals share a vocabulary so that there are both legal and moral obligations, duties, and rights; all municipal legal systems reproduce the substance of certain fundamental moral requirements." [46] Hart recognizes that law is best understood as a branch of morality or justice.[47] But he does not see morality as the only source of law.

In his book, *"The Concept of Law,"* Hart writes:

"There are many different types of relation between law and morals and there is nothing

---

[45] Hart et al., *The Concept of Law*, 7.

[46] Ibid.

[47] Ibid.

which can be profitably singled out for study as the relation between them."[48]

The previous quote suggests that Hart is not impressed with the relationship between morals and laws, at least with obligation. Hart notes:

> "It cannot seriously be disputed that the development of law, at all times and places, has in fact been profoundly influenced both by the conventional morality and ideals of particular social groups, and also by forms of enlightened moral criticism urged by individuals, whose moral horizon has transcended the morality currently accepted."[49]

Hart suggests that we could understand the law as a tool that resulted from the different moral views that permeate a particular social environment. He also relies on the likelihood that morality might not be universally understood. Hart further hints at the existence of unique kinds of morality which are not necessarily compatible.

Hart's arguments suggest that some moral values are of higher importance or of higher standard than others. Put differently, morality is stratified, or at least it has a hierarchy. This view presumes that some groups have a much higher moral ground to make laws, while others have a higher leaning (or responsibility) to obey such

---

[48] Ibid., 185.
[49] Ibid.

laws. Hart notes that throughout human history and in all places, similar groups influenced the expansion of law.

Hart does not deny the role of morality in creating laws. But this distinguished legal theorist also has an unconventional approach to the origins of laws. Apart from morality, Hart argues that laws are the product of social rules.

Hart's arguments give the impression that they are based on the effects of rules, just rules, in creating laws in society. According to Hart's, morals have little or nothing to do with obligation. It is not clear where Hart was heading in his proposing these ideas. He did not clarify what he meant in his major publications or in other works on the issue. I do not share Hart's views.

I espouse a different approach *vis-à-vis* Hart. With his positions on the utility of natural law, I fervently oppose his views. It is undeniable that morality is the essence of artificial laws. However, where did the notion of morality originate? Let us explore further.

Morality and Law

While evaluating Hart's chief arguments, I wondered whether there could be rules in society without a moral understanding. It is not clear to what extent there is a clear dissociation between morality and rules. Whether a rule is just, fair, right, or wrong, it has to be inspired by notions of morality or moral ideals.

Could we speak of rules (whether they are just) without evoking morality? Could there be laws without a clear standard of conduct, which such laws aspire to uphold? Answers for both questions could be no. But that does not imply any certainty in that assessment.

Just like Joseph Raz, H. L. A. Hart's arguments seem ambivalent about the role of morality in instilling laws in society. I am not convinced that rules are independent of moral ideals. Hart could not have it both ways.

This is to foreshadow that either society comes from certain rules, which are independent of the creation of the social environment, or the development of such rules resulted from the organization of society. To reiterate the *"Chicken and egg dilemma"* outlined in the preceding chapter, the development of rules led to the creation of society, or the creation of society led to the development of rules. A valid contention is that morality would have played a significant role in that creation.

It is not clear to the degree to which there could be laws in society without a moral patron. The nature of laws is the understanding that certain conducts are immoral. Therefore, such conducts must be restricted. Any argument to the contrary might be considered analytically shortsighted or logically fraudulent.

The Role of Social Rules

What would social rules seek to conduct if they do not conform to a higher standard? But if we are talking about standards, it should be true that such standards must come from somewhere. The question is where these standards could come from. What could the source of these standards be other than notions of morality?

The only overarching *locus* where views about what is acceptable or not come from could stem from the notion of natural law itself. Hart cannot speak of rules, laws, or social practices without referring to a greater credence to morality and, by extension, natural law, as now understood. We also note that the notion of natural law emanated from various schools of thought. But it may not be necessary to address this facet of the debate.

It would not be far-fetched to say that morality plays a more prominent role in legal obligation whether legal theorists, such as Hart and Raz want to admit it. That morality is the foundation of all artificial law. By it, setting up a clear divide between *natural law* and *positive law* in legal obligation is a futile effort.

The intellectual merit of the debate over natural law and positive legal ideas is lost in semantics. Meanwhile, an obligation is fixed, just as moral. Thus, moral values are determined by men. They are also enforced by them.

A man is only the *grantor* and *grantee* of all moral values on earth. As long as men live in social arrangements, they could obligate themselves to what they want or wish. That does not mean that what one man wants is what every man wishes.

I challenge the pervading belief that what one man wants is the same as what every other man might want.

NATURAL LAW

Modern civilizations are based on this understanding. In making this claim, it is not clear whether this approach to humanity is sustainable.

The destiny of humankind reflects the wants, the fancy, and the wishes of a few men. Such a power of the act (or power of fact) does not make of the human existence a preordained experience. What one man wants or what a few men might want is not a universal reality for humankind. Nature will take over. The natural balance will be restored.

The reason of one person about the world does not represent how all men might view their world. This continuous struggle is the essence of human reality. Some men will always strive to undermine the collective will. They will always seize the authority that the collective places in them. They will exert the power of the few on the many. But they will do so to the harm of the collective. There is no way around that reality. This is the essence of the political (if not societal) struggles that characterize most modern social settings.

To go back to the issue at hand, let us say that the notion of reason is a narrow spectrum of the world. But having laws that are specifically tailored or designed to enforce such a view is a misfortune for humanity. That we (humans) want to be stacked like sardines in a cage-like environment, which is governed by rigid rules, which are also outside our immediate control, is laughable.

Every man is expected to conform to the wants or the wishes of a few. Thus, there is always an obligation to

NATURAL LAW

obey the law. Such an obligation may not result from pure reason. Let me explain this assertion further.

Every reasonable man would deny any forms of social rules and laws that do not benefit him directly. The capacity to reason would prevent any man from being bound by the will of another. If every man could reason independently or if every man could reason own his own or for his own, there would be no society. Hence, there would be no laws; there would be no god. At least every man would have his own god.

If that were to be the case, the being would have his sets of laws. He would set up his own sets of moral values. He would answer only to himself. Because of that reality, there would be no conventional morality.

Could we say that the previous claim is not that far-fetched? The answer is yes. However, this is not the nature of a social setting. A society is supposed to prevent the man from being his own god. It stops the being from responding to his nature.

Citizen control is the nomenclature of our present world. The being could not be unless he is in a certain way. The person could not exist unless he exists according to certain expectations, which some people believe have divine origins. These expectations always come from the men themselves. This is true for both religious and secular social environments.

6. ASSESSING VIEWPOINTS

Grasping a legal obligation requires a deep understanding of what law is in its most epistemological sense. But assessing *"what law is"* is the most pressing undertaking in legal theory. For years, finding the right answer has attracted the interests of lawyers.

Even though most men and women of letter approach obligation from a similar analytical prism (that is, *natural law* versus *positive law*), few of them would recognize the linearity in the arguments, which many often evoke to disagree other viewpoints. There are hardly any disagreements in the literature on this issue.

There are nuances and shades of argument in the debate. Most often, views converge about whom is obligated in society. However, views seldom diverge about whom enforces the law or who has the authority to enforce the law.

Let us examine the claims expressed by several theorists about legal duties, although in summation here. These thinkers include, but are not limited to, John Austin, Hart, Hans Kelsen, and Joseph Raz to make sense of the idea that obligation is inherent in men.

John Austin

This legal scholar centers his arguments on the role of rights. Austin marks the line between positive and natural law. As a positivist, Austin argues that laws should be viewed as commands (commands of the sovereign).[50] Austin believes that actions (or activities) that we could not classify as commands could not fall under what we might consider as laws.[51]

From Austin's viewpoint, only general commands count as laws. Austin suggests that only the commands that emanated directly from the sovereign could be positive laws. For him, legal duties are defined and understood based on the extent of sanctions.

Austin is credited as the father of legal positivism. He is also regarded as the original framer of modern jurisprudence. His works are valued in various literary

---

[50] John Austin, *Austin: The Province of Jurisprudence Determined*, ed. Wilfrid E. Rumble, 1st edition (Cambridge ; New York, NY: Cambridge University Press, 1995).

[51] Wacks, *Understanding Jurisprudence*.

circles. For many of Austin's followers, his words are biblically proportional to legal positivism. The Austinian approach to legal positivism has a permanent imprint on various facets of modern jurisprudence, notably in Western civilizations.

Austin notes four notable features of commands, which include wish, sanction, expression of a wish, and generality.[52] But those features make up the basic beliefs for obligation. According to Austin, a command that emanated from a political superior or a sovereign automatically creates an obligation for the politically inferior members of society.[53] The duty to obey, Austin suggests, is based in the possibility for sanctions. Since we could regard the political superior or sovereign as an omnipotent lawgiver, the political inferior always owes obedience.

H. L. A. Hart

Many observers consider Hart as one of the intellectual pillars of modern jurisprudence, in the western world. This scholar assesses the notion of political obligation from a different angle. Hart also evaluated the notion of rights. But he did so within the context of a legal

---

[52] Austin, *Austin*; Wacks, *Understanding Jurisprudence*.
[53] Austin, *Austin*; Wacks, *Understanding Jurisprudence*.

obligation. Hart sees an obvious distinction between cooperation and obligation.[54]

Hart is not convinced that the law is coercive. He believes that the law is a social phenomenon, which we could understand only through social practices.[55] There is a tension in Hart's arguments about morality and society.

Hart believes that rules are necessary in society. He also recognizes the natural law. Hart further notes that because of human vulnerability and frailties, there is a need for rules that protect people and property.[56]

Even if Hart were to reject the notion that morality would the only source of law. Something else creates the law. For Hart, the law is a system of rules, which is there to ensure that promises are kept, and the sanctity of society is protected.

Hart further argues that social rules impose obligation.[57] The claim in this case or the inescapable inference here is that there is no relationship between rules and morals. Hart argues that rules vary from morality, games, and obligation rules that imposes duties.[58]

Hart rejects the notion that rules are commands. He argues that a legal system needs a valid obligation rule,

---

[54] Wacks, *The Philosophy of Law*.

[55] Hart et al., *The Concept of Law*.

[56] Ibid.

[57] Ibid.

[58] Wacks, *The Philosophy of Law*.

which must be obeyed by members of society.[59] But Ronald Dworkin argues that the law contains a solution to every social problem. Dworkin's argument centers on the view that there is more to laws than just rules.[60] Obligation is always expected in any social setting.

Hans Kelsen

This prominent scholar introduced norms as the best approach to understanding law and, by extension, legal duties. For Kelsen, a norm as something that ought to be (or ought to happen).[61] The claim here is that with obligation, a person ought to behave a certain way. The norms dictate the most suitable way of doing things. We could also say that the norms are not autonomous.

For Kelsen, norms must be sanctioned by another norm, which must be approved by a higher norm in the system.[62] Unlike Hart, Kelsen does not subscribe to the notion that rules dictate human conducts. Kelsen put forward the notion that social norms are the key to understanding human conduct. But such an argument also suggests that there ought to be a point of departure in the creation or the setting up of any social norm.

---

[59] Hart et al., *The Concept of Law*.

[60] Wacks, *The Philosophy of Law*.

[61] Kelsen, *General Theory of Law And State*.

[62] Raymond Wacks, *Law: A Very Short Introduction*, 1 edition (Oxford ; New York: Oxford University Press, 2008).

NATURAL LAW

Where such a point of departure would be? How did the notion of norms come about? What led to its universal adoption?

It is not clear of the degree to which a single approach to the origins of norms could explain the reality human beings face in their world. There is no universal way to approach the origins of norms. The logical assumption is that developing social norms is irrefutably a subjective effort.

Kelsen further argues that all norms are about the individual (or the group) under consideration.[63] Since a true norm could be hard to decipher, we must presume its existence. The problem is that such a presupposition is selective and arbitrary.[64] It might not be wrong to claim that norms are socially set up tools of control and compulsion.

Joseph Raz

This scholar is an acclaimed positivist in his own right. Many observers consider Joseph Raz as one of the recent waves of thinkers that seek to revive "The moral foundation of natural law."[65] Raz notes that the identity and the existence of legal systems could emanate from

---

[63] Ibid.
[64] Ibid.
[65] D'Entrèves and Nederman, *Natural Law*.

three elements. They include efficacy, institutional character, and sources.[66]

Just like Hart and Austin, Raz believes that the law does not depend on morality. He argues the law is autonomous.[67] Thus, as by Raz's view, we could see the law without interjecting notions of morality.[68]

According to Raz's, social factors, mostly institutional factors, may decide the origin of laws. Raz argues that the existence and the content of law may be determined by a factual inquiry about conventions, institutions, and the intents of participants in the legal system.[69] We could also say that a law is never a moral judgment; it is always a matter of tangible fact.

Despite the contentions outlined in the preceding chapters, the concept of legal obligation remains muddy, at least intellectually. Finding the meaning of law or deciphering the true meaning of various legal ideas about legal duties is a continuous (if not a futile) intellectual exercise. Many scholars seem invested in identifying flaws in the propositions of the other.

No one scholar could claim ownership over a particular legal theory. Subjectively, any theory could claim to explain what law is or what stems from legal duties. But that does not mean that such an approach would yield an accurate depiction of the subject.

---

[66] Wacks, *Understanding Jurisprudence.*

[67] Raz, *Authority.*

[68] Ibid.

[69] Ibid.

NATURAL LAW

Assessing the accuracy of these theories from an objective slant might be impracticable. To that extent, the right answer for the question posed earlier, "What is law," remains unclear. It is a daunting task. In the same vein, merging agreements about what forms a law or legal obligation remains a chimerical effort.

You might still find the subject confusing. The views I echoed here might not be enough to clarify the issues. You might say that the book is barely making a dent in the debate.

This work is only a summary of the literature. It is a hodgepodge of views and claims about legal obligation. But the book does not cover the issues extensively. The book is not exhaustive. If you would like to learn more, see my other work on the subject.

SECTION 4

The Nature of Obligation

7. OBLIGATION AS A MORAL NECESSITY

We often describe the notion of legal obligation as a moral need to obey the laws of society. But the term obligation is used to describe a duty, which could be political or moral. John Simmons notes that the terms obligation and duty are more or less the same.[70]

The most important facet of obligation, Hart further argues, is that it needs rights and power.[71] While a legal right is an interest that creates an obligation, a legal power is a mechanism that affords the ability to create or to

---

[70] A. John Simmons, *Moral Principles and Political Obligations* (Princeton, NJ: Princeton University Press, 1981).
[71] Hart et al., *The Concept of Law*.

adjust duties. [72] Put differently, power trumps rights anytime and anywhere.

It is not clear whether a legal right precedes power or vice versa. The current debate centers on whether all laws create an obligation or a duty.[73] An important question is whether there is a difference between duty and political obligation.

Simmons argues that there is an obvious distinction between the two terminologies.[74] Political obligation, for instance, is concerned with "moral requirements to act in certain ways in manners political."[75] Thus, we could understand duties as moral needs. But the term *moral need* is confusing. The extent to which such an understanding is the foundation of legal obedience remains elusive.

Moral Obligation and Consent

When we speak of obligation, we seldom think about the role of will or consent. But they are essential elements to consider; they may explain the *"reason"* or "reasons" that we provide to us about when, why, or why we obey the law. The presumption is that where there is will or consent, there could be no duties.

---

[72] Dennis Patterson, ed., *Philosophy of Law and Legal Theory: An Anthology*, 1 edition (Malden, MA: Wiley-Blackwell, 2003).

[73] Ibid.

[74] Simmons, *Moral Principles and Political Obligations*.

[75] Ibid., 12.

The literature suggests that the duty to obey the laws of society does not require a will or consent. But attaching the notion of consent or "a will" to the notion of obligation seems misguided. That could lead to more problems than it helps to clarify the literature, one might say.

Consent is incompatible with obligation. A person should not be able to decide why, when, or how he obeys the law. Such an approach could annul any sense of obligation to the laws in effect.

Under the vestige of a few legal theories, we are likely to equate the notion of legal obligation as a moral inclination or a duty to perform, to avoid, or to recognize a particular act. Could there be any political association without consent? The answer is no. But Yves Simon notes, organizing governments need consent of the governed.[76]

The understanding here is that political association is an act of reason. Such an act could also reveal a will. The argument worthy of note is that "society is not brought about by instinct and infra-rational forces but by rational judgment and free will."[77]

What is a moral obligation then? The answers are not succinct. One thinker sought to disentangle the debate. John Finnis sought to answer the noted question from a natural law paradigm.

---

[76] Yves R. Simon, *Philosophy of Democratic Government* (Notre Dame: University of Notre Dame Press, 1993).
[77] Ibid., 191.

NATURAL LAW

Many people consider Finnis a member of the recent wave of thinkers seeking to reestablish how natural law is important in "Mainstream legal and political philosophy." [78] Finnis refers to moral obligation as "practical reasonableness." He further argues that the term "moral" is confusing; it is of "somewhat uncertain connotation."[79] Passing laws are considered a practical need.

This approach to obligation centers on the need to address social problems. [80] Obligation is more sophisticated than that. Most observers believe that authority or obligation is not necessarily the result of compulsion. But this argument is a failure. Either way, if compulsion does not induce obligation, will, or consent certainly does.

Compulsion and Morality

There is a chasm between compulsion and morality. But this logic may lead to an interesting dilemma. For instance, could there be compulsion without morality? What is the purpose of morality if not to impose a way of being in the world? The answer is not clear. The logical assumption is that, if morality must be imposed, then it is

---

[78] D'Entrèves and Nederman, *Natural Law*, xxiii.

[79] Finnis, *Natural Law and Natural Rights*, 15.

[80] Ibid.

coercive. The foundation of morality, as one might also foreshadow, is both positive and coercive.

It is not clear whether morality is a free agent. Theoretically speaking, one person alone could not set up his own view of morality. One person alone could not settle the role of morality in any social setting.

The notion of morality must precede anything else. They determined that notion than any other forms of understanding. Therefore, anyone who defies acceptable moral views could experience challenging times.

Members of the society could chastise the individual. They could smear him. They could rebuke him. Members of society could treat the individual disparagingly. There is no way around the notion that morality is coercive. It is the product of man for man. This is so always and, in all places, including religious and secular social settings.

Morality is not natural. It could never be associated with the laws of nature. But in summary, just as with any artificial law, morality is also posited.

Why should we pay attention to this issue at this stage of the book? We have addressed various aspects of the obligation. But theories abound about the role of morals in obedience. An obligation cannot be discovered without assessing the role of morality. Morality cannot be assessed without incorporating the role of compulsion. Thus, these ideas go together.

It may not be necessary to recognize the term obligation as an independent factor; a legal obligation is usually the result of a particular event, context, or

NATURAL LAW

situation. There should be an instrument or a tool that induces obligation. Morality is understood as an independent intellectual mechanism, though its scope is based on a universal understanding.

We could view morality as the catalytic force that motivates or prevents an individual from engaging in certain conducts. Put differently, morality is, more often than not, the forerunner of human conduct. It is only logical to infer that views about morality can be linked to obligation.

Morality as an Elusive Idea

John Finnis argues that the notion of morality is an elusive idea. He believes that this term is a utopian ontological understanding of what the world could be or ought to be.[81] There is the notion that the term morality symbolizes an ideal world where every entity enjoys an uncontestable state of virtue, which is necessary for grasping social justice and peace.[82]

It is unlikely that nature is the forerunner of moral ideals. The extent to which the laws of nature and the laws of men, which emanated from humanity's idealistic understanding of the wilderness, are similar. The laws of man are inconsequential.

---

[81] Ibid., 297.

[82] Spooner, *Natural Law, Or, The Science of Justice*.

It is unlikely that natural law (as an epistemological idea) is the study of *the natural*. Many observers believe that it is the study of *the rational*. But that view only makes sense by separating *nature* from *the natural*. In reality, nature is a part of everything men know. Still, it is not everything men could know. It is not everything there is to know.

Natural law is not a study of the laws of nature. This argument presumes that there are no laws which could have any effect on a man's conduct. This view also presumes that once a man reaches the end of nature, he may become his own master. Nature has no relevant control over his actions or omissions. But this understanding is scandalous.

Suggesting that nature has no scope on men is a way of deifying men without calling them mini gods. This is a way of separating men from their nature. This is a way of positioning men as the only heirs of God himself (if God there is) in the wilderness. Thus, men are in charge of their own conduct in the world. I contest that belief.

Men could not be God for themselves. The ability to control one's way of being in the world is only possible through nature. Nature does not afford its creations such a feat. Still, the view is that men can regulate their conducts with their ability to reason. This assessment is likely in error.

NATURAL LAW

It is unclear the degree to which natural law is the study of reason.[83] The problem here is that the extent to which reason is a distinct human trait is no clear. It is also unclear whether the capacity to reason does not stem from human nature. But John Finnis suggests the opposite.

For Finnis, reason is independent of human nature. The sole purpose of reason is to distinguish right from wrong. This is such a narrow perspective of the way nature works. This is also a mistaken understanding about the way human beings interact with the natural environs.[84] Let us examine this view closer.

The Position of Morality

Moral ideals must have had a point of origin. It is not clear whether such moral understandings come from reason or whether reason results from morality or norms. Any norm is societal. By it, such norms must be designed and enforced.

Hans Kelsen notes that true norms must be set up. It would not be far-fetched to foreshadow that notions of morality are incompatible with nature. On that basis, we could not speak of the laws of nature in the same breath as the notion of morality.

---

[83] Oxford Conversations, *John Finnis*.

[84] Please, refer to the book titled *"Cogito, Ergo Philosophus"* to learn more about the subject.

NATURAL LAW

Nature does not impose standards of being in the world. Even if it did, such standards would not come from individual presuppositions or collective appreciations of virtue. Nature does not know virtue. Everything in nature or every natural conduct could be right or wrong, depending on the context in which such a thing, or such a conduct, is being understood.

An obligation by morality is unnatural. It is as telling a lion that it is wrong to kill a zebra; it is as telling a squirrel that it is wrong to hide its food away from other squirrels, who might starve to death; it is as impugning guilt on a cow or a horse for emptying the savanna, which was filled with grass the night before.

Even if you were to tell those beings that their conduct in the wilderness was wrong, they would not understand you. They do not know morality; they do not have morals, which men could manipulate at will.

Let us take that argument further. What sets a man apart from an animal? Please, spare me the cliché, we are reasonable animals. This argument has run out of steam; it is empty of any relevant intellectual poignancy. It is epistemologically exhausted, thus, no longer has any merit, just to put it mildly.[85]

We are animals. This reality is irrefutable. This view of ourselves has never been denied by any sound-minded intellectual. But there are implications.

---

[85] See the text titled *Cogito, Ergo Philosophus*, to learn more about this understanding.

NATURAL LAW

If we are animals, then we are also akin to other entities, which we consider animals in the most intrinsic sense. For instance, we do not differ from the bovines, the cows, the horses, and the lions, to name a few. Certainly, we have our peculiarities. But this does not mean that we are exogenous entities in nature. That means that we do not enjoy any state of preference in nature. What we do as a species is what we can do. We respond to our nature.

Human nature is like that of other living entities in the world. Just like the bovines and horses of the natural environment, we must eat. We may have to behave in a certain way to find food. We may also have to survive among the other entities that might seek to consume us.

We may have to behave in ways that other entities might consider bad for them. In effect, we are afraid of the world. We are also afraid of ourselves in the natural environment. Morality is a device which allows us *to be* in a certain way, while we prevent others (that is, human beings) from being like that, above all when it might damage our beingness.

Despite the previously stated reality, human beings are more likely to answer to their nature, rather than inhibiting it. We are inclined to find means to survive, rather than compromising our beingness. But these traits are incompatible with being in a social arrangement. Morality becomes the perfect instrument to undermine human nature. This is not a natural law.

NATURAL LAW

Any laws, designed by men and enforced by them, would be against their own nature. Thus, obedience to artificial laws must be imposed. This obligation is also coercive. It is that way at birth. A moral obligation is devoid of any inherence. Human beings are not inclined to obey human-made laws on their own choosing or of their own will.

NATURAL LAW

8. PURITY IN THE WORLD

The idea of morality presumes that there is an underlying purity in the world. Moral notions propose that human beings can reach a balance between right and wrong. We could understand that state of utmost perfection. Moral axioms proclaim the possibility of discovering the highest quality of human behavior.

Before we bridge the last portion of the manuscript, a flaw in logic is worth pointing out. If every human being were to be awarded with the capacity to reason and to settle a clear distinction between what is right and what is wrong, then why would there be laws? Why would there be a *Plan B* to obedience, as Hart suggested?[86] If human beings could inherently arrive at purity in the world

---

[86] Please, refer back to chapter 3 (The Purpose of Laws) to learn more.

NATURAL LAW

through reason, the question worth asking is why there would be a need for adopting moral standards.

If we could prove the idea of justice all the time and in any manner, why would there be a need to enforce existing laws? Why would it be necessary to require human beings to be just in their conducts, actions, and omissions? Why would it be necessary to impose a way of life which is based on rules and laws, many of which are cruel? It is not clear how to approach these questions objectively.

Our reality is irrefutable. We live under a legal regime. The extent to which such an organization is religious (or secular) is inconsequential with our obligation to the laws it produces. The kinds of laws emanating from the sovereign are not negotiable. The citizen is expected to obey; he is expected to abdicate his inherent right *to* allow the law to take its course. Nature has nothing to do with obedience.

The most fundamental question worth asking here is why we obey even though we often disagree with the laws in effect. It is not clear of a suitable answer. I must also point out that many observers have advanced several theories, namely our capacity to reason, to explain the reason we are rational beings, which is supposedly the foundation of our district nature. Thus, the presumption is that we obligate ourselves to obey, as we are intrinsically inclined to do so. We must obey our own rules. But this understanding is preposterous.

The D'Entrèvesian Approach

The view that stands out in the literature is sketched in the acclaimed text, *Natural Law: An Introduction to Legal Philosophy* (1994). Alexander Passerin d'Entrèves writes: « Mankind is a universal community or cosmopolis. The law is its expression. Being approved by the sovereign Lordship of God, it is eternal and immutable. » [87] D'Entrèves relates the doctrine of natural law, as explained in Cicero's Republic (*see* Cicero: De re Publica, 1928).[88]

The earlier view suggests that law is a natural phenomenon. It is that way because there is a universal standard of existence in the world. D'Entrèves notes, "The law is right reason in agreement with nature; it is of universal application, unchanging and everlasting; it summons to duty by its commands and averts from wrong-doing by its prohibitions." [89] This is a narrow perspective about the laws of nature. This is not to sound insolent. But I fervently reject this perspective.

Why must the need for obedience be coached, induced, and imposed? The answer is not clear. I am uncertain of the degree to which human beings are

---

[87] D'Entrèves and Nederman, *Natural Law*, 26.
[88] To learn more about Cicero's view on natural law, see the text titled De re Publica. Cicero, *Cicero: De Re Publica*, trans. Clinton W. Keyes (Cambridge, Mass.: Harvard University Press, 1928).
[89] D'Entrèves and Nederman, *Natural Law*, 25.

NATURAL LAW

inherently obedient. There is always a need for laws (often drastic rules) in society.

Despite the noted claims, it is important to understand or perhaps to discover the reason laws must be enforced. Is it because social laws are both just and unjust (that is, depending on the social context)? It is not clear that there is a perfect way to answer this question.

An obvious reality is that notions of virtue must be construed by members of society. Morality is set up by men. Thus, morality is positive, just as is the notion of positive law.

The notions of morality set up the foundation on which human civilizations stand. Still, several scholars argued that we could understand the world without a moral lens.[90] But is it even possible to envisage a world empty of morality? The answer could be no.

The existence of society or social rules depends on morality.[91] We could have no society without a larger moral framework. Despite what most scholars believe, it would be inconceivable to deny the effects of morality in the development of laws, rules, and institutions.

---

[90] Authors like John Austin, H. L. A. Hart, and Joseph Raz argue that we could understand laws without interjecting morals.

[91] Simon, *Philosophy of Democratic Government*; Finnis, *Natural Law and Natural Rights*.

Political Obligation

Political duties are requirements that every member of society must adhere to or obey. For example, performing certain acts or omitting that is non-optional. One approach to political obligation is the notion of sanction or penalty.[92] The understanding here is that individuals are compelled to act or omit to act based on the possibility of a penalty. John Austin further notes that penalty reinforces duties; it does not instill them.[93]

According to Hart, an obligation is rule-based.[94] John Austin argues that sanctions create the circumstance for people to perform or omit a certain act, when they are subject to a practiced social rule, which needs an act or omitting an act.[95] Both thinkers agree that there is always an obligation to obey the law. This is true whether that obligation is based on some specific rules or some specific sanctions (or sanction mechanisms).

Austin's argument suggests that obligation must be reinforced by a social pressure to conform, even though such a pressure might lead to a clash between the goals of the individual and his or her interests.[96] A legal duty is only valid when it is reinforced by sound moral reasons

---

[92] Austin, *Austin*.

[93] Ibid.

[94] Hart et al., *The Concept of Law*.

[95] Austin, *Austin*.

[96] Green, "Legal Obligation and Authority."

NATURAL LAW

to comply.[97] A system of rules alone does not create obligation; sanctions must go with those rules.

Authors like, John Austin, Ronald Dworkin, and Joseph Raz note that Hart's approach to political obligation is incomplete.[98] These thinkers believe that obligation is not dependent on social practices. Other legal scholars also evoked the notion of norms to explain the source of legal obligation.

It is hard to make a clear distinction in the current debate. Hart's approach, for instance, applies to certain (if not some specific) instances, namely in situations where there is a universal need for conformity.[99] To say it again, I am not convinced that there is a clear divide between social norms and social rules.

The most logical conclusion is that the current literary conversation is marred with contradictions. Another valid argument worth echoing is that we could see current evaluations about political obligation as incomplete. Thus, a better approach is needed in the present literary conversation.

So long as legal theorists, scholars, and experts in jurisprudence view positive law as separate from natural law (as now understood and not as should be understood), a succinct understanding of what is law, what is obligation, who is obligated to laws and who should be obligated to laws would be impossible to

---

[97] Ibid.
[98] Ibid.
[99] Ibid.

discover. The issues are more complex in the present context.

The best way to explore the notion of obligation is by closer examining the idea of justice. The precept also includes the notion of morality. This is the only way to understand the implications of laws in society.

Justice and Obligation

We often view the idea of justice as separate from legal duties. Hans Kelsen, for example, notes, "Law and justice are two unique concepts."[100] The notion of justice may also weaken obligation.

Most observers suggest that, under set laws, obligation is omnipresent. It may not be necessary to refute that position. Kelsen notes, "Law as distinguished from justice is positive law."[101]

The question is whether there could be an obligation to law without the presence of justice, or at least an understanding of it. Hart might say no. He might do so by echoing his views about unjust rules. Both Austin and Raz would take a similar stance, as there could be no sanctions or legitimate authority without making out justice.

Justice is a creation of natural law; justice stems from reason. Here, the entire foundation of positive law

---

[100] Kelsen, *General Theory of Law And State*, 5.
[101] Ibid.

crumbles under the weight of notions applying to morality.

When we speak of justice, the presumption is that every law must be just, at its core, at least to create an obligation. But it is frequently understood that consent may irrevocably lead to obligation. Still, this is not always the case.

Consent could be implicit; otherwise, it must be specified (or clarified). This approach to the issue is clear in Joseph Raz's argument about moral reasoning. Kelsen further notes, "There are legal orders which are, from a certain point of view, unjust."[102] There could be no obligation without justice. In addition, there could be no opinion of justice without moral reason or morality.

The idea of "will" hinges on the role of morality in individual assessment of what is just or compulsory. Justice and obligation could only co-exist when moral views play a greater role in assessing what is made out as just or unjust. What is just is what one considers it to be. It could be what a group agrees that such justice is or could be. Thus, other men are expected to uphold that view of the world.

Mine and Thine (Lysander Spooner)

Lysander Spooner eloquently notes that every just law is also unjust. He notes that morality could play a significant

---

[102] Ibid.

role in the notion of justice. Spooner further argues that justice is a suitable tool for understanding social equities, with rights, human, and property rights. Spooner refers to the idea of morality as the science of *"mine and thine."*[103] We often describe this approach as the science of justice.[104]

We could say that both justice and morality are not universally understood or comprehensively construed. An activity or a conduct some may consider as just, others may see such an activity of conduct otherwise or (simply) unjust. Although we often evoke morality as a valuable tool for justice and fairness in society, some scholars, above all positivists, struggle with the idea that morality is quintessential for having laws.

While I understand Spooner's position, I do not believe that morality and positive law disagree with each other. The problem is that most positivists agree that justice plays a significant role in the obligation. They cannot have it both ways.

To reiterate my previous assertion, there could be no justice without morality. Morality implies that natural law, as now understood, plays a greater role in legal duties. There is no obvious distinction between artificial laws and natural laws, at least as the present intellectual model depicts these two ideas. But let me disentangle these two ideas based on my understanding.

---

[103] Lysander Spooner (Legal Treaties, 1800–1926). Natural Law, Chapter 1. Spooner, *Natural Law, Or, The Science of Justice.*
[104] Ibid., 5.

Natural Law

The next chapter summarizes the gist of the arguments this text seeks to convey about the scope of natural law and positive law. It is important to distinguish between the laws of nature and the laws of men. While the arguments echoed throughout the text are reinforced by a sound analysis, let me wrap up the discussions further.

9. NATURAL LAW VERSUS POSITIVE LAW

There is an obvious difference between natural law and the laws of nature. We could understand the term "natural" as the law of things in nature. This means that nature preordained its creations in a certain way. That is the nature of these things or these entities, whether they are alive, inert to the naked eye, or subtle to the human touch. The term natural law also means something else.

Many people often use the term natural law to describe inherent human conduct in society. There are certain things that are inherently right or wrong. For example, a person shall not deprive another of life, freedom or liberty, and any other amenities. From that

NATURAL LAW

conceptualization of natural law, we might get the notion of justice. What is just is also right. The opposite is also true, some might say. Everything that is right is irrefutably just.

The Capacity to Reason

Why would an ordinary human being choose the virtue of anything else? For most scholars, the answer lies in the person's ability to reason. However, the notion of reason involves both nature and society. Thus, an irrefutable inconsistency is obvious.

Why can human beings' reason and why can the lions, the tigers, the snakes, and any other entity within the natural environment not? The answer is simple. There is no evidence that human beings alone are awarded with the capacity to reason in nature, if reason is an inherent human characteristic.

Reason could lead to both good and bad. If we could understand the capacity of a person to reason as the foundation of virtue, it would also be true that the same ideal would set a pedestal on which evil lives. But nature knows neither good nor evil. Every conduct (whether good or bad) that prolongs survival also prolongs the natural milieu.

Someone decided what a reason is or what it should be. Any idea of justice is a human set up. Along the way, this view becomes the foundation of human civilizations.

Clearly, that does not make such a view of the world a natural view.

The laws of nature, one might say, are much more complex than the precept stated previously. We could understand the laws of nature as the way conducts are defined in the natural environment. A fish may never fly. However, a bird might swim like a fish, though if it could do so, it would only be temporary.

We could understand the essence of natural law as the limits that nature imposes on its beings. Certain entities are limited in their conduct. They are also limited in their being within the natural environment.

We could understand the notion of positive law as an artificial device. The idea stemmed from the notion that human beings are reasonable beings. Their actions are based on their ability to do the right thing.

What does that mean in practice? It means that anyone who engages in conduct that does not fall in line with socially accepted behaviors is wrong. The individual must receive a punishment for engaging in such conduct. This is the essence of positive law. Laws were made to regulate their own conducts. But the justification for such laws is that "everyone would abide by them." The expectation is that everyone should.

Apart from this view being absurd, it is also dangerous. It provides men a reason to do and to omit from doing with little or no consequences, moral, or else. So long as we consider a conduct moral, it is acceptable. It is justifiable. But the opposite claim is also true.

Let us say that every person must obey any laws, which members of society consider moral. The belief is that such laws are just and, by extension, moral. The person could be right from wrong. This is illogical.

Any positive law is irrefutably the law of men. Such an approach to laws has little or nothing to do with nature itself. Of the term "positive," for example, it comes from the verb posit, which implies a position. Someone or some entity put something or someone in a position. Thus, positive laws are the laws that men set for themselves. Else, it could be the laws that some men set forth doe others. Nature has little or nothing to do with it.

Limit Versus Restriction

Using the term *"Nature"* in this book is to rebuke the nation that men are governed by a higher instance. That instance is God. We often use the terms divine laws and natural laws interchangeably.

For natural law, nature and God are not necessarily the same entity. For instance, the laws of nature regulate and limit conducts. The laws of God or the laws of men generate and restrict conducts.

Is there an obvious distinction between limitation and restriction? The answer is yes. Limitation allows the conduct to take place. It may also place a limit on the degree to which it happens.

Let us say that it is against a man's nature to fly like a bird. That does not mean that a man could not be airborne. The issue here is that nature would never allow a person to function like a bird in the sky. Even if a person could be airborne, nature would not allow that individual to function like a bird in the sky.

The term restriction is not a natural idea. No one or nothing is restricted in nature. The term also implies that a conduct is not limited outside the boundaries of nature itself. But such conduct is always restricted.

Let us take the earlier example of a flying bird to make the case that nature imposes limits, while artificial laws impose restrictions. Although a person might find a means to be in the air, there may be a law that restricts anyone from being in the air.

Suppose that Karl invents a gadget that allows him to fly. Karl may not have permission to use that gadget wherever and whenever he chooses. There might be a law that restricts the use of gadgets in certain areas. Failure on his part to obey such laws could cause his sanctions, which could lead to his imprisonment. Karl knows that he must (always) obey such a law.

Key Arguments

A duty to obey the law is never inherent. It must come from an imposition. Such a burden, as I sought to show throughout this manuscript, often emanates from social norms, which are reinforced by social rules and other

NATURAL LAW

forms of sanctions. To present an interesting argument in defense of my contention, it became necessary to assess the essentiality of the term legal obedience. I accomplished this aim by echoing existing viewpoints regarding a person's natural leaning to obey the law.

It was vital to examine the role of morality in creating obligation. The book explored, though briefly in this case, the role of reason in inciting or fermenting legal duties. Still, an obligation to comply with artificial laws is never natural. A legal obligation is always expected. It is always compulsory. In any circumstance, such an obligation must come from somewhere. It must be induced; it must be imposed; it must be enforced.

Legal duties are often the results of positive legal doctrines. However, such duties are inherently coercive. It may not be accurate to equate such duties as natural leanings or an inherent duty in men to comply with any form of commands or anything conjured up by others.

It was important to explain how positive laws stem from social rules. It was necessary to describe such rules as the laws that often emanate from social institutions. Considering the ideas noted here, every law so designed, so enforced, and so rationalized by men is also the law of men. This is true regardless of their origins.

It was important to point out that theories about the origins of *artificial* laws are ambiguous. It became urgent to sort out discrepancies in the literature. In this context, I tried to make the case for a better approach to grasping natural law and, by extension, positive law.

FINAL WORDS

Closing Thoughts

CONCLUSION

The primary goal set forth in this project was to introduce a more practical approach to the notion of natural law. It was paramount to recenter the debate. Another goal was to offer an alternative approach in the conversation about the extent of legal obligation in society. Of course, my idiosyncrasies are based primarily on personal reflections and my authentic life experience.

The views that I explained throughout this text stem from personal viewpoints about what a legal obligation is or what such an understanding should entail. It was important to layout that facets of the subject are often overlooked or even under-explored. It was vital to note that the literature is too complex. The goal was to change that literary dynamic in this paperback.

NATURAL LAW

The success of this work may depend on your appreciation of the views echoed in it. However, this work is not exhaustive. While this is a pertinent piece of literature, it may not be broad enough to satisfy your intellect. Considering this is a short compilation, it was important to outline my views on the subject as succinctly as possible.

My contention is that the term natural law is misunderstood. The literature is permeated with erroneous assumptions about the concept. It was necessary to present an alternative side of the debate. It was vital to mark down the intellectual territory, which I sought to defend in this discipline.

Although the literature suggests that positive law and natural law are two different legal doctrines, these concepts are often understood in similar contexts. In fact, they have similar effects. It was essential to stress that both ideas stem from ideals describing the laws of men. It was intellectually justified to highlight that there is always an obligation to obey the law. But the legal obligation to relinquish oneself to a blinded obedience is not necessarily natural, at least not at its core.

As we end this *tête-à-tête*, the issue remains the same. Did the views echo here are potent enough to sway you one way or another? Were the arguments offered here forcefully to compel you to see the issues differently, assuming that you did not originally share the views echoed in the manuscript?

NATURAL LAW

It would be presuming on my part to suggest that the present opus is the *end-all-be-all* reference on the subject. I certainly hope that you could glean a lot from this literary journey. I also hope that you share the view that this work could affect the literature positively.

It is worth reiterating that the ideas echoed here are not the results of the research. They did not stem from any empirical study. Likewise, they did not emanate from an in-depth examination of the subject. This is not a book review, although the text referenced several works by a few prominent authors in the field.

This book did not set out to explore a specific point or an issue in the literature. It was not designed to be in depth. This work is not a review of the literature. Instead, this book was a synthesis of several works that explored legal obligation. This text is also the result of several essays, many of which I compiled many years ago.

Popular sentiments about natural law are in error. The present discourse is tainted, considering that few works have explored the concept of natural law outside the realm of a positive legal maxim. The views presented in the present context are concise and genuine. This was an invitation for further analysis.

The views conveyed in this collection of essays are unique; they embody my understanding of the term natural law. That being noted, this was not a futile intellectual effort. I hope that the book will incite your interest in natural law. However, keep a positive outlook about the topic even after reading the manuscript.

NATURAL LAW

Despite the downsides of this short volume, the goal was to instigate a deeper awareness of the concept of natural law. Untangling the notion was a complex task. If you would like to learn more about the subject, see my other works, which are more thorough. They are listed toward the end of the document.

BIBLIOGRAPHY

Anderson, Stephen R. "How Many Languages Are There in the World?," 2010. https://www.linguisticsociety.org/content/how-many-languages-are-there-world.

Austin, John. *Austin: The Province of Jurisprudence Determined.* Edited by Wilfrid E. Rumble. Revised ed. edition. Cambridge ; New York, NY: Cambridge University Press, 1995.

———. *The Province of Jurisprudence Determined and The Uses of the Study of Jurisprudence.* Indianapolis, IN: Hackett Publishing Company, Inc., 1998.

Bastiat, Frederic. *The Law.* New York, N.Y.: Cosimo Classics, 2007.

Cicero. *Cicero: De Re Publica.* Translated by Clinton W. Keyes. Cambridge, Mass.: Harvard University

NATURAL LAW

     Press, 1928.

Denning, Alfred. *The Discipline of Law*. 1 edition.
     London: Oxford University Press, 2005.

D'Entrèves, Alexander Passerin, and Cary J. Nederman.
     Natural Law: An Introduction to Legal Philosophy.
     New Brunswick, N.J: Routledge, 1994.

Entrèves, Alessandro Passerin d'. *Natural Law: An
     Introduction to Legal Philosophy*. 3 (reprint).
     Transaction Publishers, 1951.

————. *Natural Law: An Introduction to Legal Philosophy*.
     2nd ed. London: Hutchinson University Library,
     1970.

Finnis, John. *Natural Law and Natural Rights*. 2 edition.
     Oxford ; New York: Oxford University Press,
     2011.

Green, Leslie. "Legal Obligation and Authority." In *The
     Stanford Encyclopedia of Philosophy*, edited by
     Edward N. Zalta, Winter 2012. Metaphysics
     Research Lab, Stanford University, 2012.
     https://plato.stanford.edu/archives/win2012/e
     ntries/legal-obligation/.

Hart, H. L. A., Leslie Green, Joseph Raz, and Penelope
     A. Bulloch. *The Concept of Law*. 3 edition.
     Oxford, United Kingdom: Oxford University
     Press, 2012.

Hill, Gerald, Kathleen Hill, and Nolo Editors. *Nolo's
     Plain-English Law Dictionary*. 1 edition. Berkeley,
     CA: NOLO, 2009.

Kelsen, Hans. *General Theory of Law And State*. 1 edition.

NATURAL LAW

Clark, N.J: The Lawbook Exchange, Ltd., 2007.

Merriam-Webster. *Merriam-Webster's Collegiate Dictionary, 11th Edition.* 11th edition. Springfield: Merriam-Webster, Inc., 2003.

Oxford Conversations. *What Is New Classical Natural Law Theory?* John Finnis: Life of Faith, 2016. https://www.youtube.com/watch?v=0N5ffOM BOZc.

Patterson, Dennis, ed. *Philosophy of Law and Legal Theory: An Anthology.* 1 edition. Malden, MA: Wiley-Blackwell, 2003.

Raz, Joseph, ed. *Authority.* New York: NYU Press, 1990.

Schmitt, Carl, and Tracy B. Strong. *Political Theology: Four Chapters on the Concept of Sovereignty.* Translated by George Schwab. 1 edition. Chicago: University Of Chicago Press, 2006.

Simmons, A. John. *Moral Principles and Political Obligations.* Princeton, NJ: Princeton University Press, 1981.

Simon, Yves R. *Philosophy of Democratic Government.* Notre Dame: University of Notre Dame Press, 1993.

Spooner, Lysander. *Natural Law, Or, The Science of Justice: A Treatise on Natural Law, Natural Justice, Natural Rights, Natural Liberty, and Natural Society : Showing ... Is an Absurdity, a Usurpation, and a Crime.* Place of publication not identified: Gale, Making of Modern Law, 2010.

Tobin, Philip Chase. *25 Doctrines of Law You Should Know.* New York: Algora Publishing, 2007.

Wacks, Raymond. *Law: A Very Short Introduction.* 1

NATURAL LAW

edition. Oxford ; New York: Oxford University Press, 2008.

———. *The Philosophy of Law: A Very Short Introduction.* Oxford ; New York: Oxford University Press, 2006.

———. *Understanding Jurisprudence: An Introduction to Legal Theory.* 2nd edition. Oxford ; New York: Oxford University Press, 2009.

INDEX

NATURAL LAW

ABOUT THE AUTHOR

BEN WOOD JOHNSON, Ph.D.

Dr. Johnson is an author, educator, and philosopher. He is a retired police officer. As a 27-year veteran of law enforcement, Dr. Johnson is a Fort Leonard Wood police graduate from the International Criminal Investigative Training Assistance Program (ICITAP). He is also a graduate from the Diplomatic Security Service (Mobile Division).

Dr. Johnson is a retired diplomatic security officer, with expertise in close protection/presidential security, intelligence, counter ambush/terrorism, anti-riot, special weapons and tactics, and national security specialist. During his police career, Dr. Johnson held various police assignments, including patrol, anti-riot, investigation, border control, special unit response team, counter

NATURAL LAW

ambush, team commander, administration, scout lead driver (presidential motorcade), advanced team, counterintelligence, translator, logistics, and training.

Dr. Johnson has taught criminal justice subjects at police academies. He has taught special operations techniques to veteran police officers. Dr. Johnson is an adjunct faculty member in criminal justice at Penn State University, Harrisburg. He holds a doctorate in educational leadership and administration. His academic background includes education, law, political science, public administration, and criminal justice. His research interests include policing in America, race and crime, law, school leadership, administration, and foreign politics.

Dr. Johnson writes about legal theory, education, public policy, politics, race and crime, and ethics. He is fluent in French, Spanish, Portuguese, and Italian. He enjoys reading, poetry, painting, and music. You may contact Dr. Johnson by e-mail or via postal services. See other information below.

E-mail: benwoodpost@gmail.com

Twitter handle: @benwoodpost

Facebook Page: @benwoodpost

Blog (Ben Wood Post): www.benwoodpost.org

Website: www.drbenwoodjohnson.com

Website: www.benwoodjohnson.com

OTHER WORKS

Selected works by Dr. Ben Wood Johnson

1. Racism: What is it?
2. Sartrean Ethics: A Defense of Jean-Paul Sartre as a Moral Philosopher
3. Jean-Paul Sartre and Morality: A Legacy Under Attack
4. Sartre Lives On
5. Forced Out of Vietnam: A Policy Analysis of the Fall of Saigon
6. Cogito Ergo Philosophus
7. Le Racisme et le Socialisme: La Discrimination Raciale dans un Milieu Capitaliste
8. International Law: The Rise of Russia as a Global Threat

NATURAL LAW

TESKO PUBLISHING

www.teskopublishing.com